Introduction for Parents

This book was written to help the most important people, children, learn about autism. I hope that being the father of an autistic child as well as a physician has aided me in giving an intimate and accurate portrayal. I also hope that parents, teachers, and other professionals will find the book useful.

Autism has become a popular topic of newspaper and magazine articles, TV talk shows, and even movies. While the attention is certainly welcome and generally well-intentioned, two troubling themes run through many of these accounts. The first is that miraculous cures are available to parents who circumvent standard therapies to discover the real cause of their child's problem. True cures are rare. What cures do occur are most often the result of having diagnosed autism where some other problem is causing autistic-like behavior. Not all strange or silent children are autistic. The second troubling theme is that autistic people have amazing powers to perform memory, mathematical, or musical feats. Such "savant" powers are uncommon.

Autism is a serious developmental disorder. It is most recently estimated to occur in 15 per 10,000 births. Childhood autism affects three areas of behavior: social relations, language development, and play activities. Its cause is usually unknown, although sometimes an infection or other problem prior to birth is documented. Chromosome abnormalities can also cause autism. Autistic behavior is generally apparent before age two, and it can often be seen much earlier in the autistic infant's resistance to cuddling and lack of smiling and eye contact.

Autistic individuals do not form normal relationships with parents, siblings, or peers. They do not seem to take an interest in people as people. Parents have difficulty comforting them. Some autistic children have a great aversion to being kissed or hugged, while others may insist on being hugged, tickled, and swung around. Even the highest functioning adults, at the very least, have problems understanding another person's point of view.

Often, autistic people have no spoken language. The mute autistic child may have little or no ability to use symbols of any kind and usually has a poor understanding of spoken words. Echoing and pronoun confusions are common in the autistic person's spoken language, as are repetition of phrases heard in the past and a ritualistic use of language. For example, one autistic child asks everyone he meets, "Can you name five companies that make greeting cards?"

Autistic children do not play with other children and seldom or never "pretend play." Instead of pretending that a toy car's engine is running, an autistic child might line up cars in a row. Spinning themselves or other objects is common, as are attachments to unexpected objects like drinking straws and repetitive activities such as leaf tearing.

Autistic children do not readily tolerate changes in their environment or schedule. Regularity in activities is usually important. For example, one autistic child insists on seeing a train whenever at a certain railroad crossing, and has a screaming tantrum unless the driver waits for one to pass.

Sensitivity to sounds, sights, and smell are also common in autistic people. For instance, the echoing sounds in a gym may cause great distress. Conversely, autistic individuals may not respond to powerful stimuli like honking horns or pain. Many are dangerously self-abusive.

While cures of autistic people are rare, much can be done to help the individual function better. Modern treatment stresses cooperation between home and school rather than institutional control. Sign language and spoken language are often used together to help the child communicate. Tangible rewards, like raisins, can be used to encourage appropriate behavior. Strict schedules and regular activities are important in controlling behavior and promoting learning.

Autistic children who have no useful language by the age of five are seldom able to ever live an independent existence. As adults, they may stay with their parents or live in a group home, sheltered workshop, or residential facility. The best outlook is for those children who have useful language and who score above 70 on an IQ test. Unfortunately, only about 20% of autistic children score that high. It is difficult to tell if children with the lower scores are retarded. They may be unable or unwilling to respond to the test items because of deficiencies in language or because of intolerance of the testing situation. Whatever an IQ score "means" in this setting, it is still highly predictive of future success.

Social behavior tends to improve as the autistic person gets older. Sometimes in adolescence, however, behaviors and skills deteriorate. Of even more concern is the development of epilepsy at this age in up to 25%. Anti-seizure medication for epilepsy and even anti-psychotic medication for behavior management may be useful. Autism, however, is definitely not a psychosis. Several medications are being investigated that affect neurotransmitters, and these have shown promise in some groups of autistic people.

In any medical condition, but especially in those like autism that are comprised of many factors, there are always individual differences. Any parent having further questions is encouraged to contact the experts in autism listed at the back of this book.

About the pictures in this book: they are natural photos of our family life. Only the concluding portrait was formally posed. How did we get Russell to stay with the group—something usually difficult for him? We rewarded him (perhaps "bribed" is more accurate) with candy while I stepped on the shutter release.

I hope children will enjoy the book. It would be great if it leads to discussions of how the Russells of the world are like them as well as different. Maybe someday some readers will become educators or researchers studying autism.

RUSSELL IS EXTRA SPECIAL

A Book About Autism for Children

by Charles A. Amenta III, M.D.

Magination Press ● *Washington, DC*

To my wife, Marie

Library of Congress Cataloging-in-Publication Data
Amenta, Charles A. (Charles Anthony)
    Russell is extra special : a book about autism for children /
Charles A. Amenta III.
        p.   cm.
    Summary: Describes the daily life, likes and dislikes, and habits
of Russell Amenta, who is a happy boy despite being severely
autistic.
    ISBN 0-945354-43-6 (cloth). — ISBN 0-945354-44-4 (paper)
    1. Amenta, Russell—Mental health—Juvenile literature.
2. Autistic children—Juvenile literature. 3. Autism—Juvenile
literature. [1. Autism. 2. Amenta, Russell.] I. Title.
RJ506.A9A63   1992
618.92'8982'0092—dc20   91-41863
                                                        CIP
                                                        AC

Manufactured in the United States of America
10 9 8 7 6 5 4 3

Russell is a special child. He is autistic. This means he is different from other children in three ways. First, he likes to be alone as much as possible. Other people do not seem to interest him very much. Second, he cannot talk, and he has difficulty understanding what other people are saying. Third, he does not always play the way other children do.

Russell is nine years old. He has two younger brothers, Benjamin and Gregory. Benjamin and Gregory love their older brother, Russell. They know he is autistic so they make an extra effort to help him and be friends with him. Like all brothers, they can have fun together. They like to take baths together.

Gregory and Benjamin sometimes ask their father why Russell is autistic. Their father is a doctor, but he does not know the answer. Nobody knows how children become autistic. Many seem to have been born that way. When they are babies *some* autistic children do not snuggle when their parents cuddle them. They lie stiffly in their parents' arms and never smile back when someone smiles at them.

Russell, like many autistic children, *did* smile and cuddle with his parents when he was a baby. Maybe that is why Russell has such a nice smile now. He likes tickling, and he still likes to cuddle with his mother.

Gregory and Benjamin like to play with friends. Russell does not. He likes to be by himself. He goes to the other side of the room or even leaves the room when other children come over. All autistic children have difficulty making friends. As they grow older, they usually become more comfortable being around other people.

Autistic children also have difficulty learning to talk properly. Many, like Russell, cannot talk at all. Some repeat whole sentences or parts of sentences like an echo. They may confuse "you" and "I." They say, "You want a cookie," when they mean "I want a cookie." Sometimes their voices sound flat and mechanical when they talk, like a robot or computer. But they can learn to speak better with help at home and at school.

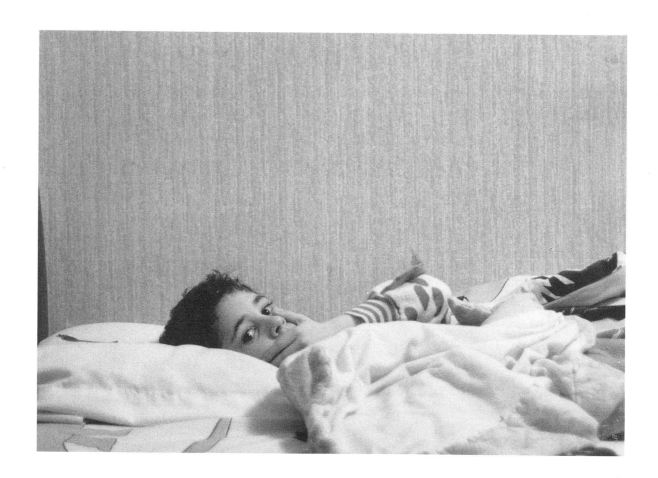

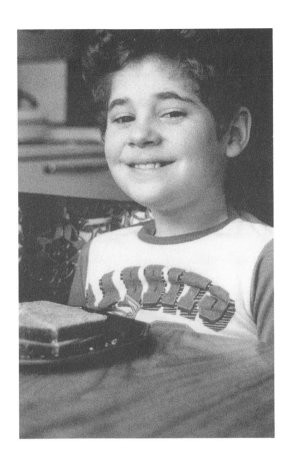

    Russell can hum, babble, laugh, and scream. Russell screams both when he is unhappy and when he is excited. Sometimes he laughs very loudly—and then screams. It is hard to understand what Russell is feeling and why his mood changes so quickly.

Russell's parents and teachers try to teach Russell sign language. He knows signs for "eat," "drink," and "more." When Russell makes his sign for "more," it looks like he is praying or clapping his hands.

Gregory and Benjamin think it is fun to sign. They can make the sign for drink much better than Russell can.

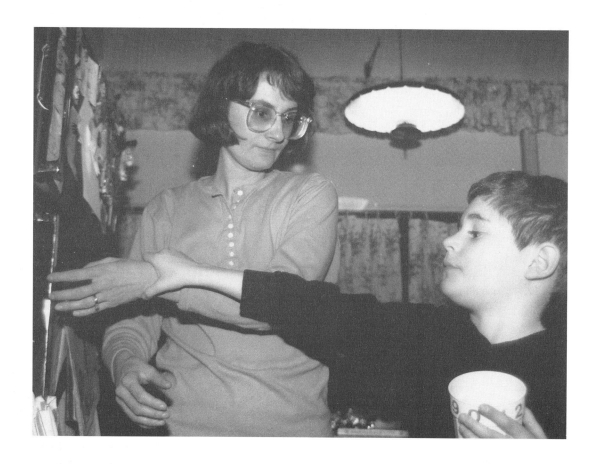

Russell does not like to sign. He would rather hand someone his cup when he is thirsty. To get a drink, sometimes he pulls his mother by her hand and puts it on the refrigerator door. Autistic children often prefer to use action to get what they want.

Russell loves to eat, but he does not have good manners. He likes to eat with his fingers. When nobody is looking, he picks the topping off the pizza and leaves the crust. He opens up his sandwich and smears the peanut butter.

Russell's parents have taught him to eat properly with his spoon and fork.

Sometimes Russell covers his eyes, pulls at his eyelids, or looks away. Maybe the lights seem too bright to him. Maybe he does not want to see the people around him. When he was one-and-a-half years old, Russell began to ignore his parents. He would not come when they called and would not look at them when they spoke to him. To encourage him to pay attention to them, Russell's parents gave him a Cheerio every time he looked at them. Rewards like this help autistic children learn. Rewards work even better when they are part of a game.

It is difficult for Russell to learn things because he is severely autistic. It took him a long time to be toilet trained and to be able to dress himself. Not all autistic children have such difficulty learning. Some are very smart. A few are even amazing. They can do things like multiplication without paper or a calculator. Others can play the piano well. Even if they are smart or talented, autistic people usually need special help. They especially need help making friends and learning to work at a job.

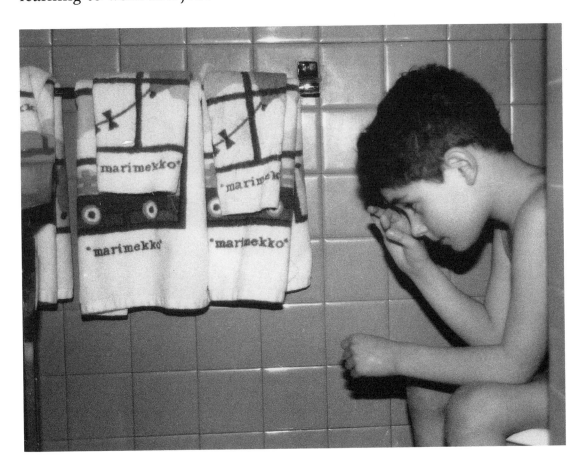

Most children learn by imitating others. They learn while they play and use their imagination. Benjamin and Gregory pretend they are conducting music like their mother does.

Gregory pretends he is a doctor like his father.

Benjamin pretends to take pictures of Russell.

Russell would rather put the toy camera in his mouth. Russell does *not* imitate other people. Autistic children do not pretend play.

The way autistic children play is often very different from other children. Sometimes they like to do things over and over and over again—like lining up toy cars. But they do not make car sounds. Some autistic children like to spin toys—even toys that are not tops. Many like shiny objects like spoons or doorknobs.

Russell has a special timer he likes to stare at. Inside the timer,
a bright green liquid flows from top to bottom.

Russell likes to carry a plastic straw wherever he goes. He folds it and pinches it between his thumb and fingers. He also likes to look out the window and tap on it with plastic toys. Sometimes he likes tapping with just his hands.

Russell's parents have help teaching Russell. Russell goes to school. He likes riding in the bus. He is in a class with other children who are like him. At school, he learns simple tasks and sign language. The teachers also help him behave better and learn to play with the other children.

There is a swing set at school. Russell *loves* swinging. All children like to rock back and forth to music and to whirl around, but autistic children usually *love* to whirl and rock. Sometimes that is their favorite way of playing.

Russell walks gracefully. He is learning to swim, and he *loves* the water. Some autistic children are not very graceful. Some are clumsy in their movements.

Autistic children can be very sensitive. Some get very upset if their schedule or anything they like is changed. They notice if a favorite chair is moved from its place — even if only a little bit. Russell wants everything to be on time, especially dinner.

Russell sometimes causes problems. He smears ointment on the wall. He eats the toothpaste. He breaks Gregory's and Benjamin's toys. That makes them very angry. Gregory makes a fist because he is angry. Behind Gregory is some wallpaper that Russell started to peel off the wall.

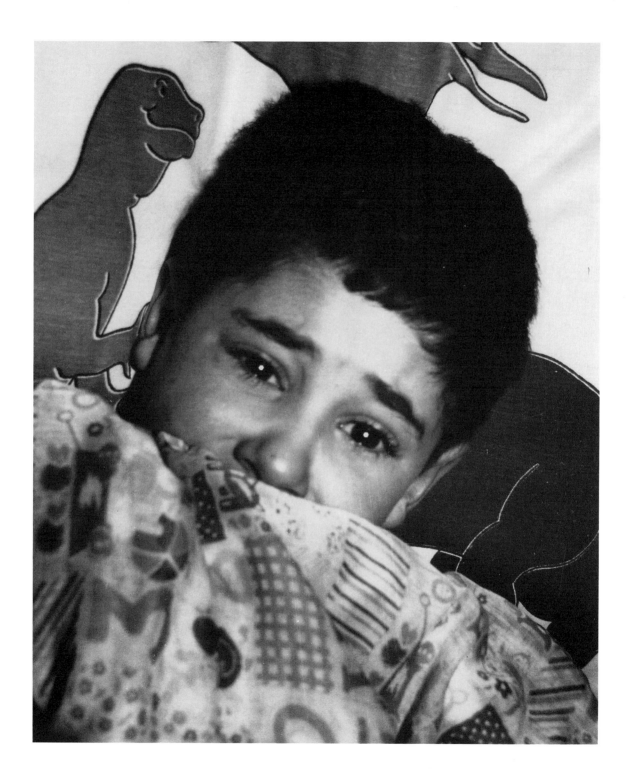

Nighttime is Russell's worst time. Sometimes he wakes up and screams even if he is not hurt. Sometimes he crys and then giggles. Sometimes he is too excited to stay in bed.

Many autistic children have problems at night. Some hurt themselves on purpose. They do not seem to care about the pain. When Russell has a tantrum, he kicks his shin with his heel. Luckily, doctors and teachers have learned new ways of helping autistic people. They can learn to stop hurting themselves.

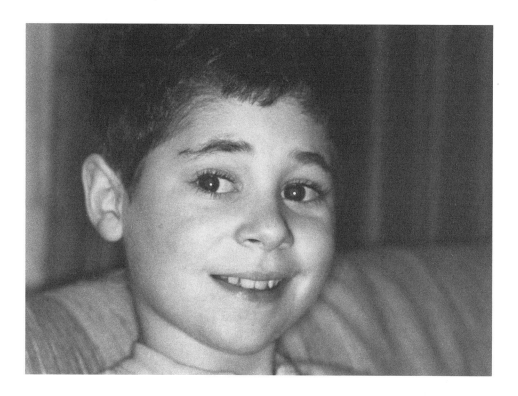

Even though he is autistic, Russell is a happy boy.

And even though Russell sometimes causes problems, Russell's family is thankful that they have him in their house. They think he is *extra* special.

Resources

Autism Society of America, 8601 Georgia Avenue, Suite 503, Silver Spring, MD 20910; 301-565-0433; FAX 301-565-0834

Donald Cohen, M.D., Yale University Child Study Center, 230 Frontage Road, P.O. Box 3333, New Haven, CT 06510

Robert L. Koegel, Ph.D., Director, Autism Research Center, Counseling/Clinical/School Psychology Program, Graduate School of Education, University of California at Santa Barbara, Santa Barbara, CA 93106

Bennett L. Leventhal, M.D., Professor of Psychiatry and Pediatrics and Director (Interim), Department of Psychiatry, University of Chicago, 5841 South Maryland Avenue, Chicago, IL 60637

Bernard Rimland, Ph.D., Autism Research Institute, 4182 Adams Avenue, San Diego, CA 92116

Eric Schopler, Ph.D., Department of Psychiatry, University of North Carolina, CB 7180 Medical School Wing E, Chapel Hill, NC 27599

Periodicals

The Advocate, Autism Society of America, 8601 Georgia Avenue, Suite 503, Silver Spring, MD 20910

Autism Research Review International, Autism Research Institute, 4182 Adams Avenue, San Diego, CA 92116

Focus on Autistic Behavior, Pro-Ed, 8700 Shoal Creek, Austin, TX 78758

Journal of Autism and Developmental Disorders, Plenum Publishing Corp., 233 Spring Street, New York, NY 10013

Books

Autistic Children: A Guide for Parents and Professionals, 2nd edition, by Lorna Wing, New York, Brunner/Mazel, 1985

Diagnostic and Statistical Manual of Mental Disorders, 3rd edition, revised, Washington, DC, American Psychiatric Association, 1987

Emergence: Labeled Autistic, by Temple Grandin and Margaret M. Scariano, Navato, CA, Arena Press, 1986

The ME Book: Teaching Developmentally Disabled Children, by O. Ivar Lovaas, Austin, TX, Pro-Ed, 1981

Mixed Blessings, by William Christopher and Barbara Christopher, Nashville, TN, Abington Press, 1989; paperback, New York, Avon Books, 1990

Videotape

Autism: A World Apart, produced by the Autism Society of Los Angeles; available from Fanlight Productions, 47 Halifax Street, Boston, MA 02130